Happily Ever After

11-13-10

Tim + Gina
Congratulations!
Enjoy your life together.
our best,
Delbert + Gina
Adams

Happily Ever After

by Helene & Jim McMullan

the

wit

and

wisdom

of

marriage

ANGEL CITY PRESS

ANGEL CITY PRESS, INC.
2118 Wilshire Boulevard, Suite 880
Santa Monica, California 90403
310-395-9982
www.angelcitypress.com

First published in 1998 by Angel City Press
1 3 5 7 9 10 8 6 4 2
FIRST EDITION
Copyright © 1998 by Helene McMullan and Jim McMullan

Design and layout by Dello & Associates, Inc., www.dello.com

ISBN 1-883318-20-3
Printed in Hong Kong

Distributed by Universe Publishing through St. Martin's Press
175 Fifth Avenue, New York, New York 10010

Library of Congress Cataloging-In-Publication Data

McMullan, Jim, 1936-
   Happily ever after : the wit and wisdom of marriage / by Jim
McMullan and Helene Slack McMullan. — 1st ed.
   p. cm.
   Includes bibliographical references (p.) and index.
   ISBN 1-883318-20-3
   1. Marriage — Quotations, maxims, etc. 2. Marriage — Humor.
   1. McMullan, Helene Slack, 1940- . ll. Title.
PN6084.M3M43 1998
306.81 — dc21   97-45374
                                                        CIP

*To our sons Sky and Tysun who enrich our
life by giving us a new understanding of love
— we thank them for never losing sight of the
importance of a stable family unit.*

table of contents:

Working on this book has been a joy and a gift for us and we'd like to acknowledge the assistance of the following individuals: first and foremost, we express our gratitude to our editor Paddy Calistro and to Scott McAuley of Angel City Press, who both shared our vision in bringing *Happily Ever After* to fruition. And thanks go, also, to Dave Matli of Dello and Associates, our talented and gifted designer, for his creative work brought another dimension to this book. To Jane Centofante whose attention to editorial detail made so much difference.

acknowledgments

To Edward McMullan for his continued encouragement and support. To all our married friends who cheered us on and stayed together through thick and thin. A special thanks to all the teachers, gurus, masters and saints who inspired us to walk toward the light and always reminded us that we were made in God's image.

Last but not least . . . a generous thank you to all the quotable people, past and present, whose inspiring words fill this book.

— Helene and Jim McMullan

"Chains do not hold a marriage together. It is threads, hundreds of tiny threads which sew people together through the years. That is what makes a marriage last."

— Simone Signoret

Afuter the celebration ends and the rice and flowers are swept away, after "I love you" and "I do" have faded into the church rafters, after the champagne and wedding cake are but a memory, after the honeymoon is over . . . one of life's great challenges begins . . . marriage.

We've been married for twenty-eight years and we're just starting to get the hang of it. After our first year of marriage with its trials and tribulations, we realized that when in doubt, being kind to each other was a sure way to heal unhappy moments. So we had the words "Be Kind" engraved on the inside of our wedding rings. Those words have helped us to get through the clutter that kept us from remembering that first and foremost we are good friends.

There's an old Irish proverb that says, "Don't walk in front of me; I may not follow. Don't walk behind me; I may not lead. Walk beside me and be my friend." We find that we are happiest when we forget we're married and notice that we are sharing our thoughts as good friends. This is a solid foundation on which to begin a journey together.

Marriage is a rewarding experience for those who are willing to persist and triumph. Like a good garden that needs constant care to maintain its integrity, a relationship needs loving care or it tends to get overrun with neglect. Constant watering and nurturing are a must. Weeding is a necessity. Those pesky intruders keep coming up, and if you're not diligent, they take over and strangle all that was thriving.

Communication has become the bedrock of our marriage. How to listen, when to talk and how much to say are questions we deal with on a daily basis. Eric Fromm tells us that, "Love is possible only if two persons communicate with each other from the center of their existence." To accomplish this miracle is a challenge, but it becomes the cornerstone of a successful marriage.

The notion of two people standing apart and coming together with combined strength is an image that has helped sustain our marriage through the years. What is the secret of allowing our mates to retain their identities and not feel it will cost us our own? The great Kahlil Gibran in his classic poem, "The Prophet," suggests that we "Fill each other's cup but drink not from one cup. Sing and dance together and be joyous, but let each one of you be alone, even as the strings of a lute are alone though they quiver with the same music."

Of all the tools in our "marriage kit," we have found the art of compromise to be one of the most valuable. As Samuel Smiles puts it, "The golden rule of married life is: 'bear and forebear.' Marriage is like government: a series of compromises. One must give and take, refrain and restrain, endure and be patient."

But sometimes we lose sight of our own identity in the process of pleasing a mate and, by trial and error, we have found that it is better to meet each other with our strengths, sharing our completeness. Simone de Beauvoir tells us that, "The curse which lies upon marriage is that too often the individuals are joined in their weaknesses rather than their strengths, each asking from the other instead of finding pleasure in giving."

Togetherness and freedom seem to be at odds with one another and might explain why so many marriages fail. Funnyman Rodney Dangerfield puts it this way, "We sleep in separate rooms; we have dinner apart; we take separate vacations; we're doing everything we can to keep our marriage together." It's a fine line that all married couples must walk: "letting there be spaces in your togetherness" and at the same time wanting closeness and intimacy. To accomplish this may seem like an impossible trick; it is the work — or better, the caring — of marriage.

An abiding faith in a spiritual power has helped to guide and govern our relationship. We like Maria McIntosh's words, "Strong are the instincts with which God has guarded the sacredness of marriage." Our religious and spiritual explorations have been the rock upon which our marriage is built. We realized, early on, that trying to solve our problems on a earthly level, though important, could only take us so far, and that to gain genuine healing, we had to let go to a higher source, allowing God to provide us with inspiration to uplift and nurture our marriage. We've taken care to find quiet moments for connecting with each other on a higher plane. We have created a foundation of trust and rapport that helps us cope with life's problems in an open and positive new way. Louis Evans reminds us that "Many a marriage could have been saved if the couple had remembered this: that their hearts belong to each other, but their souls belong to God."

In the seventeenth century women were considered property and played roles subservient to their husbands. In the nineteenth century women were not viewed as enticing unless they brought property or wealth to the marriage. In the twentieth century women carved a new and independent place for themselves both inside and outside the matrimonial state. As we move into the twenty-first century it looks as if the spiritual revolution will elevate marriage to a new level where men and women will learn to respect and love their mates from an entirely new perspective. When two people from different backgrounds come together with conflicting values, dreams, opinions and ambitions, it's always gratifying when things work out. As the comic philospher Bill Cosby sees it, "For two people in a marriage to live together day after day is unquestionably the one miracle the Vatican has overlooked." We have found that striving for a common goal and working as a team, with mutual support, while allowing our most beloved friend the space to create and dream his or her own dreams, has pointed us in the right direction.

Over the years we've discovered that our marriage has mellowed and matured. A series of zig-zag moves through mazes, hurdles and pitfalls strengthened us and allowed us to be survivors. When the smoke finally lifted, we looked back and thanked our lucky stars that we had the courage and the stamina to stay with our marriage. When you survive, together, as we have, you realize that a new, tender love emerges and you realize, too, that it's stronger and more durable than that of the young and simple-hearted lovers who began their innocent journey so long ago. We now know that Booth Tarkington was speaking directly to us when he said, "It is love in old age, no longer blind, that is true love. For love's highest intensity doesn't necessarily mean its highest quality."

So here is a book full of ideas by people who have definite opinions about marriage. Most have either made one work or screwed up one. They may have watched from the sidelines or joined the game in full battle gear. These observations and quotations come from all viewpoints: serious, sarcastic, facetious, loving and critical. Here for your pleasure and enjoyment is a mixed bag of images and notions to chew upon and mull over. We're glad to be able to bring together so many different viewpoints about an institution that is the centerpiece of life.

We wish you persistence, fortitude, imagination, dexterity and most of all a sense of humor. And if you do decide to embark on this very entertaining adventure, remember the wise words of Leonardo da Vinci, "When creating a fine piece of sculpture, you keep chipping away all the useless fragments until you discover the magnificent work of art within." We think marriage is a lot like that.

united

"A happy marriage perhaps
represents the ideal of human
relationship — a setting in
which each partner, while
acknowledging the need of the
other, feels free to be what he
or she by nature is; a relationship in which instinct as well as
intellect can find expression;
in which giving and taking are
equal; in which each accepts
the other."

— Anthony Storr

"My wife was an immature wom
taking a bath, and my wife wou
sink my boats."

"A man would prefer to come home to an unmade bed and a happy woman than to a neatly made bed and an angry woman."
— Marlene Dietrich

"A marriage is based on full confidence, based on complete and unqualified frankness on both sides; they are not keeping anything back; there's no deception underneath it all. If I might so put it, it's an agreement for the mutual forgiveness of sin."
— Henrik Ibsen

"A person of genius should marry a person of character. Genius does not herd with a genius."
— Oliver Wendell Holmes

"All happily married people have managed to accept the fact that marriage is no better and no worse than any other human institution. Also, perhaps even more important, they have learned to accept themselves and each other for what they really and honestly are."
— Ernest Havemann

would be home in the bathroom,
lk in whenever she felt like it and

— Woody Allen

"It is the man and woman united that makes the complete human being. Separate she wants his force of body and strength of reason; he her softness, sensibility and acute discernment. Together they are most likely to succeed in the world. A single man has not nearly the value he would have in that state of union. He is an incomplete animal. He resembles the odd half of a pair of scissors."

— Benjamin Franklin

"If you are afraid of loneliness do not marry."

— Anton Chekhov

If ever two were one, then surely we.
If ever man were lov'd by wife, then thee;
If ever wife was happy in a man,
Compare with me ye women if you can.
I prize thy love more than whole mines of gold.
Or all the riches that the East doth hold.
My love is such that rivers cannot quench,
Nor ought but love from thee, give recompence.
Thy love is such I can no way repay,
The heavens reward thee manifold I pray.
Then while we live, in love let's so persevere,
That when we live no more, we live ever.

— Anne Bradstreet *"To My Dear and Loving Husband"*

"It ought to be illegal for an artist to marry . . . If the artist must marry let him find someone more interested in art, or his art, or the artist part of him, than in him. After which let them take tea together three times a week."

— Ezra Pound

"What makes a happy marriage? It is a question which all men and women ask one another. The answer is to be found, I think, in the mutual discovery by two who marry, of the deepest need of the other's personality and the satisfaction of that need."

— Pearl S. Buck

"Love means giving one's self to another person fully, not just physically. When two people really love each other, this helps them to stay alive and grow. One must really be loved to grow. Love's such a precious and fragile thing that when it comes we have to hold on tightly. And when it comes, we're lucky because for some it never comes at all. If you have love, you're wealthy in a way that can never be measured. Cherish it."

— Nancy Reagan

"If you have respect and consideration for one another, you'll make it."

— Mary Durso

"Coming together is a beginning; keeping together is progress; working together is success."

— Henry Ford

"Marriage is a ceremony in which rings are put on the finger of the lady and through the nose of the gentleman."

— Herbert Spencer

"There is no greater excitement than to support an intellectual wife and have her support you. Marriage is a partnership in which each inspires the other and brings fruition to both of you."

— Millicent Carey McIntosh

"We sleep in separate rooms; we have dinner apart; we take separate vacations; we're doing everything we can to keep our marriage together."

— Rodney Dangerfield

"We were in 'like' with each other for a long time before we were in love. Being in 'like' gets you through the bad patches when love is strained."

— John Gregory Dunne

"When you make the sacrifice in marriage, you're sacrificing not to each other but to unity in a relationship in which two have become one."

— Joseph Campbell

"Marriage is a lottery in which men stake their liberty and women their happiness."

— Madame de Rieux

"Marriage: A long conversation checkered by disputes."

— Robert Louis Stevenson

"When two people are of one in their inmost hearts, they scatter even the strength of iron or bronze and when two people understand each other in their inmost hearts, their words are sweet and strong like the fragrance of orchids."

— I Ching

"I have great hopes that we shall l
our lives as much as if we had never r

"If it weren't for marriage men and women would fight with total strangers."

— anonymous

"Marriage is an alliance of two people, one of whom never remembers birthdays and the other who never forgets them."

— Ogden Nash

"Marriage is not merely sharing the fettuccine, but sharing the burden of finding the fettuccine restaurant in the first place."

— Calvin Trillin

"The curse which lies upon marriage is that too often the individuals are joined in their weaknesses rather than their strengths, each asking from the other instead of finding pleasure in giving."

— Simone de Beauvoir

"The difficulty with marriage is that we fall in love with a personality, but we must live with a character."

— Peter De Vries

h other all
d at all."
— Lord Byron

"May you grow old
on one pillow."
— Armenian proverb

wives

WIVES TAKE HUSBANDS | chapter two

"Let woman then go on not asking favors, but claiming as a right the removal of all hindrances to her elevation in the scale of being; let her receive encouragement for the proper cultivation of all her powers, so that she may enter profitable into the active business of life. Then in the marriage union, the independence of the husband and wife will be equal, their independence mutual, and their obligation reciprocal."

— Lucretia Mott

"Say what you will, making marriage work is a woman's business. The institution was invented to do her homage; it was contrived for her protection. Unless she accepts it as such — as a beautiful, bountiful, but quite unequal association — the going will be hard indeed."

— Phyllis McGinley

"A man's wife has more pow

"A good wife is heaven's last best gift to man; his angel and minister of graces innumerable; his gem of many virtues; his casket of jewels; her voice his sweet music; her smiles his brightest day; her kiss the guardian of his innocence; her arms the pale of his safety, the balm of her health, the balsam of his life; her industry, his surest wealth; her economy, his safest steward; her lips his faithful counselors; her bosom, the softest pillow of his cares; and her prayers, the ablest advocates of heaven's blessings on his head."

— Jeremy Taylor

If you want to be loved
For the rest of your life,
Be more of a woman
And less of a wife.

— Susan Anderson

"Only two things are necessary to keep a wife happy. One is to let her think she is having her way, and the other is to let her have it."

— Lyndon B. Johnson

"A girl must marry for love, and keep on marrying until she finds it."
— Zsa Zsa Gabor

"My wife dresses to kill. She cooks the same way."
— Henny Youngman

er him than the state has."
— Ralph Waldo Emerson

Wives are young men's mistresses, companions for middle age, and old men's nurses.
— Francis Bacon

An ideal wife is any woman who has an ideal husband.
— Booth Tarkington

We lose more women to marriage than war, famine and disease.
— Cruella de Vil

Behind every successful man there is a woman telling him he doesn't amount to much.
— Mark Twain

"Nobody objects to a woman being a good writer or sculptor or geneticist as long as she manages also to be a good wife, mother, good looking, good tempered, well dressed, well groomed, unaggressive."

— Marya Mannes

"There are two kinds of women; those who want power in the world and those who want power in bed."

— Jacqueline Bouvier Kennedy Onassis

"Marriage? Fun? Fun for men you mean."

— Scarlett O'Hara

"By all means marry; if you get a good wife, you'll become happy; if you get a bad one, you'll become a philosopher."

— Socrates

"Most of the beauty of women evaporates when they achieve domestic happiness at the price of their independence."
— Cyril Connolly

"Women will never be as successful as men because they have no wives to advise them."
— Dick Van Dyke

"The trouble with some women is they get all excited over nothing and then they marry him."
— Cher

"The great question . . . which I have not been able to answer is, what does a woman want?"
— Sigmund Freud

"Life has a way of evening things up. For every woman who makes a fool out of some man, there's another who makes a man out of some fool."
— anonymous

"No matter how happily a woman may be married, it always pleases her to discover that there is a nice man who wishes she were not."
— H.L. Mencken

"These impossible women! Ho
was right; can't live with them

"If you want to know about a man, you can find out an awful lot by looking at who he married."
— Kirk Douglas

"It seems that the bride generally has to make more effort to achieve a successful marriage than the bridegroom."
— Elizabeth Post

"To catch a husband is an art; to hold him is a job."
— Simone de Beauvoir

"I chose my wife as she did her wedding gown, for qualities that would wear well."
— Oliver Goldsmith

"There's nothing like a good dose of another woman to make a man appreciate his wife."
— Clare Boothe Luce

"To our wives and sweethearts: may they never meet."
— anonymous

ey do get around us! The poet
thout them."

— Aristophanes

"Women may be whole

oceans deeper than we are,

but they are also a whole

paradise better. She may

have got us out of Eden,

but as a compensation she

makes the earth very

pleasant."

— John Oliver Hobbes

"Here's to woman! Would that falling into her hands."

"A man who desires to get married should know everything or nothing."

— George Bernard Shaw

"I never married because I have three pets at home that answer the same purpose as a husband. I have a dog that growls every morning, a parrot that swears all afternoon, and a cat that comes home late at night."

— Marie Corelli

"When you meet someone who can cook and do housework — don't hesitate a minute — marry him."

— Joey Adams

"It was a mixed marriage. I'm human, he was a Klingon."

— Carol Leifer

"Women have a right to work wherever they want to as long as they have dinner ready when you get home."

— John Wayne

uld fall into her arms without

— Ambrose Bierce

"Men are always doomed

to be duped, not so much by the

arts of the other sex as by

their own imaginations.

They are always wooing

goddesses and marrying

mere mortals."

— Washington Irving

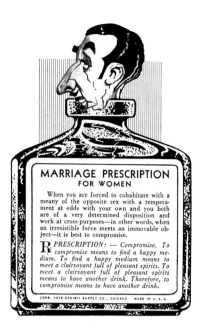

MARRIAGE PRESCRIPTION
FOR WOMEN

When you are forced to cohabitate with a meany of the opposite sex with a temperament at odds with your own and you both are of a very determined disposition and work at cross-purposes—in other words, when an irresistible force meets an immovable object—it is best to compromise.

℞ *PRESCRIPTION: — Compromise. To compromise means to find a happy medium. To find a happy medium means to meet a clairvoyant full of pleasant spirits. To meet a clairvoyant full of pleasant spirits means to have another drink. Therefore, to compromise means to have another drink.*

COPR. 1938 EXHIBIT SUPPLY CO., CHICAGO   MADE IN U.S.A.

MARRIAGE PRESCRIPTION
FOR WOMEN

He's a wise-guy and know-it-all-type. Even when he's wrong, he won't admit it. When things have gone wrong for you during the day, don't expect a soft shoulder to lean on because all you will get is a bony elbow, or a bunch of fives. He has a great line. You fell for it, but after you're married, he will throw out the same line to every girl he meets, much to your embarrassment.

℞ *PRESCRIPTION:—A good resolution is like the chorus girl—easy to make but hard to keep.*

COPR. 1938 EXHIBIT SUPPLY CO., CHICAGO   MADE IN U.S.A.

"Last week I told my wife a man is like wine, he gets better with age. She locked me in the cellar."

— Rodney Dangerfield

"The only thing that holds a marriage together is the husband being big enough to step back and see where his wife is wrong."

— Archie Bunker

"A man in the house is worth two in the street."

— Mae West

"The best way to get your husband to do something is to suggest that he's too old to do it."

— Anne Bancroft

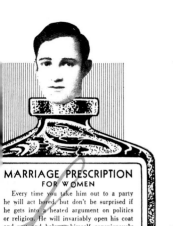

MARRIAGE PRESCRIPTION
FOR WOMEN
Every time you take him out to a party
he will act bored, but don't be surprised if
he gets into a heated argument on politics
or religion. He will invariably open his coat
and vest and balance himself conspicuously
on the two back legs of his chair at the
dinner table. If drinks are served, he will
guzzle far more than his share, and immedi-
ately after dinner will flop down in the most
comfortable chair, and go to sleep.

℞ *PRESCRIPTION: — Be nonchalant.*
Reach for a pickle instead of a sweet.

COPR. 1938 EXHIBIT SUPPLY CO., CHICAGO   MADE IN U.S.A.

"Nothing flatters a man as

much as the happiness of his

wife; he is always proud of

himself as the source of it."

— Samuel Johnson

"No man can either live piously or die righteously without a wife."
— Johann Paul Richter

"Men are nicer to the women they don't marry."
— Belle Livingstone

"Married men live longer than single men, but married men are
a lot more willing to die."
— Johnny Carson

"My most brilliant achievement was my ability to be able to
persuade my wife to marry me."
—Winston Churchill

"Being a husband is a whole-time job. That is why so many husbands fail. They cannot give their entire attention to it."
— Arnold Bennet

"When I said I would die a bachelor, I did not think I should live till I were married."
— William Shakespeare, *Much Ado About Nothing*

"Marriage is a mistake every man should make."
— George Jessel

"When you decide to marry someone, go have lunch with his ex-wife."
— Shelley Winters

"The cocks may crow but it's the hen that lays the egg."
— Margaret Thatcher

"If I was the best man at her wedding, why'd she marry him?"
— Al B. Merton

"Never strike your wife, even with a flower."
— Hindu proverb

"Husbands are chiefly good as lovers when they are betraying their wives."
— Marilyn Monroe

"If men knew how women pass the time when they are alone, they'd not marry."
— O. Henry

"The husband is always the last to know."
— English proverb

"Husbands are like fires. They go out if they are unattended."
— Zsa Zsa Gabor

"Marriage is like twirling

a baton, turning hand-

springs, or eating with

chopsticks; it looks so easy

till you try it."

— Helen Rowland

"Marriage may often be a storm a muddy horsepond."

"Marriage is like pantyhose. It all depends on what you put into it."
— Phyllis Schlafly

"Deceive not thyself by over-expecting happiness in the married estate. Remember the nightingales which sing only some months in the spring, but commonly are silent when they have hatched their eggs, as if their mirth were turned into care for their young ones."
— Thomas Fuller

"Marriage is a wonderful institution. But who would want to live in an institution?"
— H.L. Mencken

"A man is in general better pleased when he has a good dinner upon his table, than when his wife talks Greek."
— Samuel Johnson

"Marriage isn't just spiritual communion and passionate embraces; marriage is also three meals a day and remembering to take out the garbage."
— Dr. Joyce Brothers

ke, but celibacy is almost always

— Thomas Love Peacock

43

"No girl who is going to marry need bother to win a college degree; she just naturally becomes a 'Master of Arts' and a 'Doctor of Philosophy' after catering to an ordinary man for a few years."

— Helen Rowland

"You marry the man of your dreams, but after fifteen years you're married to a reclining chair that burps."

— Roseanne Barr

"The institution of marriage in all societies is a pattern within which the strains put by civilization on males and females alike must be resolved, a pattern within which men must learn in return for a variety of elaborate rewards, new forms in which sexual spontaneity is still possible and women must learn to discipline their receptivity to a thousand other considerations."

— Margaret Mead

"Dishwater helps to keep a wedding ring bright."

— anonymous

"Marry an orphan; you'll never have to spend boring holidays with the in-laws . . . at most an occasional visit to the cemetery."

— George Carlin

"Keep thy eyes wide open before marriage, and half shut afterwards."

—Benjamin Franklin

"For two people in a marriage to live together day after day is unquestionably the one miracle the Vatican has overlooked."
— Bill Cosby

"Marriage is neither heaven nor hell; it is simply purgatory."
— Abraham Lincoln

"There is nothing worse than solitude, growing old without a shoulder to lean on. Marry, marry even if he's fat and boring!"
— Coco Chanel

"A good marriage is like a casserole, only those responsible for it really know what goes into it."
— anonymous

"I've always loved my wife, I've always loved my children, I've always loved my grandchildren, and I've always loved my country."
— Dwight D. Eisenhower

"Marrying a man is like buying something you've been admiring for a long time in a shop window. You may love it when you get it home, but it doesn't always go with everything else in the house."
— Jean Kerr

"Never go to bed mad. Stay up and fight."
— Phyllis Diller

"Marrying a man is like having your hair cut short. You won't know whether it suits you until it's too late to change your mind."
— Jane Goodsell

"We all suffer from the preoccupation that there exists in the loved one — perfection."
— Sidney Poitier

"A successful marriage is not a gift, it's an achievement."
— Ann Landers

"It takes patience to appreciate domestic bliss; volatile spirits prefer unhappiness."
— George Santayana

"Marriage: a market which has nothing free but the entrance."
— Michel de Montaigne

"Love is an ideal thing, marriage a real thing; a confusion of the real and the ideal never goes unpunished."
— Johann Wolfgang von Goethe

"Keep the delights of your love evergreen and growing by planting their roots deep in truth and watering them in wisdom."

— anonymous

Carte postale – ¿Pos

"Women speak because they wish to speak; whereas a man speaks only when driven to speech by something outside himself — like, for instance if he can't find any clean socks."

— Jean Kerr

"I told my wife the truth. I told her I was seeing a psychiatrist. Then she told me the truth; that she was seeing a psychiatrist, two plumbers and a bartender."

— Rodney Dangerfield

"The first year he talks and she listens. The second year she talks and he listens. The third year they both talk and the neighbors listen."

— Donald McGill

"A man loves to think that he has done it all himself; and the wife smiles, and lets it go at that."

— James M. Barrie

"My wife was too beautiful for words, but not for arguments."

— John Barrymore

To keep your marriage brimming
with love in the marriage cup,
whenever you're wrong, admit it;
whenever you're right, shut up.

— Ogden Nash *"A Word to Husbands"*

"Husbands think we should know where everything is. He asks me, 'Roseanne, do we have any Cheetos left?' Like he can't go over to the sofa cushion and lift it himself."

— Roseanne Barr

"If you want your spouse to listen and pay strict attention to every word you say, talk in your sleep."

— anonymous

The course of true love
Will smoothly run soon
If the very last coarse
Is a fine Dessert Spoon.

TWO DESSERT SPOONS

"Take it from me, marriage isn't a word; it's a sentence."

— King Vidor

"All married couples should learn the art of battle as they should learn the art of making love. Good battle is objective and honest — never vicious or cruel . . . Good battle is healthy and constructive and brings to a marriage the principle of equal partnership."
— Ann Landers

"Edith, stifle yourself."
— Archie Bunker

"Married couples who love each other tell each other a thousand things without talking."
— Chinese proverb

"A husband should tell his wife everything that he is sure she will find out, and before anyone else does."
— Thomas Robert Dewar

"When a man brings his wife flowers for no reason — there's a reason."
— Molly McGee

"If your wife is small, stoop do

"A husband should not insult his wife publicly at parties. He should insult her in the privacy of his home."
— James Thurber

"Marriage is a two-way proposition, but never let the woman know she is one of the ways."
        — W.C. Fields

"An occasional lucky guess as to what makes a wife tick is the best man can hope for. Even then, no sooner has he learned how to cope with the tick than she tocks."
        — Ogden Nash

"She contradicts me even when I don't say anything!"
        — Bill Hoest

"Marriage is really tough because you have to deal with feelings and lawyers."
        — Richard Pryor

"You know, all that stuff I call men — 'hot slabs of meat,' 'love slaves,' 'pigs' — that's all affectionate."
        — Judy Tenuta

ıd whisper in her ear."
        — Jewish proverb

"Marriage is an alliance entered into by a man who can't sleep with the window shut, and a woman who can't sleep with the window open."

— George Bernard Shaw

"The difference between a successful marriage and a mediocre one consists of leaving about three or four things a day unsaid."

— Harlan Miller

"Everything that irritates us about others can lead us to an understanding of ourselves."

— C. G. Jung

"Remember, a woman wins an aged husband by listening to him, and a young man by talking to him."

— William H. Browne

"Love is possible only if two persons communicate with each other from the center of their existence."

— Erich Fromm

"What greater thing is there for two human souls than to feel that they are joined. . . to strengthen each other. . . to be at one with each other in silent unspeakable memories."

— George Elliot

"I had some words with my wife, and she had some paragraphs with me."

— anonymous

"There are but two objects
in marriage, love or money.
If you marry for love, you
will certainly have some very
happy days, and probably
many very uneasy ones; if for
money, you will have no
happy days and probably no
uneasy ones."

— Philip Dormer Chesterfield

"You should never kiss a girl until you have enough bucks to buy her a ring and her own VCR, 'cause she'll want to have videos of the wedding."

— Allan (age 10)

"It is a truth universally acknowledged, that a single man in possession of a good fortune, must be in want of a wife."

— Jane Austen

"A successful man is one who makes more money than his wife can spend. A successful woman is one who can find such a man."

— Lana Turner

"Marriage is primarily an economic arrangement, an insurance pact . . . one pays for it in dollars and cents, always at liberty to discontinue payments . . . woman's premium is a husband, but she pays for it with her name, her privacy, her self-respect, her very life, 'until death doth part.' "
— Emma Goldman

"They say I married my wife because her uncle left her a whole lot of money. That's not true. I would've married her no matter who left her the money."
— Spanky McFarlin

"The husband who wants a happy marriage should learn to keep his mouth shut and his checkbook open."
— Groucho Marx

"An extravagance is anything you buy that is of no use to your spouse."
— anonymous

"No woman marries for money; they are all clever enough before marrying a millionaire, to fall in love with him first."
— Cesare Pavese

"Before marriage, a man yearns for the woman he loves; after marriage, the 'Y' becomes silent."
— anonymous

"My wife and I have the satisfaction that every dime we've got is honestly ours. I should say this, that Pat doesn't have a mink coat. But she does have a respectable Republican cloth coat, and I always tell her that she would look good in anything."

— Richard M. Nixon

"Beware the woman who knows the cost of everything and the value of nothing."

— English proverb

"A fool and his money are soon married."

— Carolyn Wells

"I played Santa Claus many times, and if you don't believe it, check out the divorce settlements awarded my wives."

— Groucho Marx

"I've had an exciting life. I married for love and got a little money along with it."

— Rose Kennedy

"I don't think I'll get married again. I'll j

"Trust your husband, adore your husband, and get as much as you can in your own name."

— Joan Rivers

"I won't say my previous husbands thought only of my money, but it had a certain fascination for them."
— Barbara Hutton

"I want a man who is kind and understanding. Is that too much to ask of a millionaire?"
— Zsa Zsa Gabor

"There is a way of transferring funds that is even faster than electronic banking. It's called marriage."
— James Holt McGavran

"Marriage halves our griefs, doubles our joys, and quadruples our expenses."
— Vincent Lean

"It is impossible to reckon how much a husband owes a wife or a wife a husband. It is an infinite debt, it can be paid only in eternity."
— Johann Wolfgang von Goethe

l a woman I don't like and give her a house."
— Lewis Grizzard

"Marriage is like a bank account. You put it in, you take it out, you lose interest."
— Irwin Corey

"It is a lovely thing to have a
husband and wife developing
together and having the feeling
of falling in love again. That is
what marriage really means;
helping one another to reach
the full status of being persons,
responsible autonomous beings
who do not run away from life."

— Paul Tournier

"Sensual pleasures

have the fleeting

brilliance of a

comet; a happy

marriage has the

tranquility of a

lovely sunset."

— Ann Landers

"Sex when you're married is like going to a 7-Eleven. There's not as much variety, but at three in the morning, it's always there."
— Carol Leifer

"Love does not consist of gazing at each other but in looking together in the same direction."
— Antoine de Saint-Exupéry

"Let there be spaces in your togetherness, and let the winds of the heavens dance between you. Love one another, but make not a bond of love; let it rather be a moving sea between the shores of your soul. Fill each other's cup but drink not from one cup. Give one another of your bread but eat not from the same loaf. Sing and dance together and be joyous, but let each one of you be alone. Even as the strings of a lute are alone though they quiver with the same music."
— Kahlil Gibran

"Men always want to be a woman's first love. That is their clumsy vanity. We women have a more subtle instinct about things. What we like is to be man's last romance."
—Oscar Wilde *"A Woman of No Importance"*

"To keep the fire burning brightly there's one easy rule: keep the two logs together, near enough to keep each other warm and far enough apart — about a finger's breath —- for breathing room. Good fire, good marriage, same rule."
— Marnie Reed Crowell

Let me not to the marriage of true minds
Admit impediments. Love is not love
Which alters when it alteration finds,
Or bends with the remover to remove:
O, no! It is an ever-fixed mark,
That looks on tempests and is never shaken;
It is the star to every wandering bark,
Whose worth's unknown, although his height be taken.
Love's not Time's fool, though rosy lips and cheeks
Within his bending sickle's compass come;
Love alters not with his brief hours and weeks,
But bears it out even to the edge of doom.
If this be error and upon me proved,
I never writ, nor no man ever loved.

— William Shakespeare (Sonnet 116)

Love, be true to her; life, be dear to her;
Health, stay close to her; joy draw near to her;
Fortune, find what you can do for her,
Search your treasure-house through and through for her,
Follow her footsteps the wide world over —
And keep her husband, always her lover.

— Anna Lewis

Come live with me, and be my love,
And we will some new pleasures prove
Of golden sands, and crystal brooks,
With silken lines, and silver hooks.

— John Donne *"The Bait"*

"Chains do not hold a marriage together. It is threads, hundreds of tiny threads which sew people together through the years. That is what makes a marriage last more than passion or even sex."

— Simone Signoret

"A good marriage is that in which each appoints the other guardian of his solitude."

— Rainer Maria Rilke

"Don't get married to an actress, because they're also actresses in bed."

— Roberto Rosellini

"Here's to the husband and here's to the wife; may they remain lovers for life."

— anonymous

"I'd like to get married because I like the idea of a man being required by law to sleep with me every night."

— Carrie Snow

"The plural of spouse is spice."

— Christopher Morley

"When two people are under the influence of the most violent, most insane, most delusive, and most transient of passions, they are required to swear that they will remain in that excited, abnormal and exhausting condition continuously until death do them part."

— George Bernard Shaw

"My wife and I have a great relationship. I love sex, and she'll do anything to get out of the kitchen."

— Milton Berle

"One of the best things about marriage is that it gets young people to bed at a decent hour."

— Morris McNeil Musselman

"Like everything which is not the involuntary result of fleeting emotion, but the creation of time and will, any marriage, happy or unhappy, is infinitely more interesting and significant than any romance, however passionate."

— W.H. Auden

"Marriages are made in Heaven a
— John Lyly

"Many a man has fallen in love with a girl in a light so dim he would not have chosen a suit by it."
— Maurice Chevalier

"What most men desire is a virgin who is a whore."
— Edward Dahlberg

"Never refer to your wedding night as the 'original amateur hour.'"
— Phyllis Diller

nsummated on Earth."

caring

"I don't know why
people should feel that
because they have
married, they may give
up all pretense of good
manners and treat their
partners as an 'old shoe.'"

— Emily Post

"There isn't time so brief as life – for bickerings, apologies, heartburnings, calling to account, there is only time for loving."

— Mark Twain

"Seldom or never does a marriage develop into an individual relationship smoothly and without crisis. There is no birth of consciousness without pain."

— C. G. Jung

"Why does a woman work for years to change a man's habits, and then complain that he's not the man she married?"

— Barbra Streisand

"Three things in human life are important: The first is to be kind. The second is to be kind. The third is to be kind."

— Henry James

"Marriage is a book of which the first chapter is written in poetry and the remaining chapters in prose."

— Beverley Nichols

"I've been married for forty-nine years and I'm still in love with the same woman. If my wife ever finds out she'll kill me."

— Henny Youngman

"A happy marriage begins when we marry the one we love, and then blossoms when we love the one we married."

— Sam Levenson

"Have the courage to listen to your wife when you should, and not to listen when you should not."

— Stanislaus Leszczynski

"Marriage is an operation by which a woman's vanity and a man's egotism are extracted without an anesthetic."
— Helen Rowland

"Love is blind, but marriage restores its sight."
— George Lichtenberg

"Once you have found her never let her go."
— Rodgers & Hammerstein *"Some Enchanted Evening"*

"Sometimes I wonder if men and women really suit each other. Perhaps they should live next door and just visit now and then."
— Katharine Hepburn

"Marriage is a science."
— Honoré de Balzac

"The golden rule of married life is: 'bear and forbear.' Marriage is like government; a series of compromises. One must give and take, refrain and restrain, endure and be patient."
— Samuel Smiles

"My mother said, 'Marry a man with good teeth and high arches.' She thought I should get that into the genetic structure of the family."
— Jill Clayburgh

"Marriage is an adventure in cooperation. The more we share the richer we will be; and the less we share the poorer we will be."
— Harold B. Walker

"What counts in making a happy marriage is not so much how compatible you are, but how you deal with incompatibility."
— George Levinger

"The best friend is likely to acquire the best wife, because a good marriage is based on the talent for friendship."
— Friedrich Nietzsche

"Marriage is like a three-speed gear box: affection, friendship and love. It isn't advisable to crash your gears and go right through to love. You need to ease your way through. The basis of love is respect, and that needs to be learned from affection and friendship."
— Peter Ustinov

"Marriage is a ceremony by which two persons of the opposite sex solemnly agree to harass and spy on each other for ninety-nine years, or until death do them join."
— Elbert Hubbard

"The heart of marriage is memories."
— Bill Cosby

"Love is not enough. It must be the foundation, the cornerstone, but not the complete structure. It is much too pliable, too yielding."
— Bette Davis

"A successful marriage is an edifice that must be rebuilt every day."
— André Maurois

"Marriage is like life in that it is a field of battle and not a bed of roses."
— Robert Louis Stevenson

"No compass has ever been invented for the high seas of matrimony."
— Heinrich Heine

"Marriage is a bribe to make a housekeeper think she's a householder."
— Thornton Wilder

"The truth is, perfect marriages don't exist any more than perfect weddings. When couples accept this, they are freed to work toward true greatness — not in detail, but in spirit and passion and love."
— Robert Fulgum

"Marriage ain't easy but nothing that's worth much ever is."
— Lillian Carter

"I'd rather live with a woman I love in a world full of trouble, than to live in heaven with nobody but men."
— Robert G. Ingersoll

"A Code of Honor: Never approach a friend's wife with mischief as your goal. There are just too many women in the world to justify that sort of dishonorable behavior. Unless she's really attractive."

— Bruce Jay Friedman

"To have and to hold from this day forward, for better for worse, for richer, for poorer, in sickness and in health, to love and cherish, till death do us part."

— *Book of Common Prayer*

"As we walked down the aisle we promised each other that we could get out of this marriage next week and not wait til death did us part. The promise was the bedrock of our marriage."
— John Gregory Dunne

"Happiness is not having what you want but wanting what you have."
— Rabbi H. Schachtel

"A good marriage, if there is such a thing, rejects the condition of love. It tries to imitate those of friendship."
— Michel de Montaigne

"Like all successful politicians, I married above myself."
— Dwight D. Eisenhower

"Happy and thrice happy are they who enjoy an uninterrupted union, and whose love, unbroken by any complaints, shall not dissolve until the last day."
— Horace

"A successful marriage requires falling in love many times, always with the same person."
— Mignon McLaughlin

"I married the first man I ever kissed. When I tell this to my children they just about throw up."
— Barbara Bush

"The first bond of society is marriage; the next, our children; then the whole family and all things in common."
— Marcus Tullius Cicero

"Each coming together of man and wife, even if they have been mated for many years, should be a fresh adventure; each winning should necessitate a fresh wooing."
— Marie Carmichael Stopes

"Come, let's be a comfortable couple and take care of each other. How glad we shall be, that we have somebody we are fond of always, to talk to and sit with."

— Charles Dickens

"Remember, that if thou marry for beauty, thou bindest thyself all thy life for that which perchance will neither last nor please thee one year; and when thou hast it, it will be to thee of no price at all; for the desire dieth when it is attained, and the affection perisheth when it is satisfied."

— Sir Walter Raleigh

"Never above you, never below you, always beside you."

— Walter Winchell

"Marriage is the proper remedy. It is the most natural state of man, and therefore the state in which you will find solid happiness."

— Benjamin Franklin

"Marriage isn't about finding the right person; it's being him."

— Jim McMullan

"My whole working philosophy is that the only stable happiness for mankind is that it shall live married in blessed union to woman-kind-intimacy, physical and psychical between a man and his wife. I wish to add that my state of bliss is by no means perfect."

—D.H. Lawrence

"When marrying, ask yourself this question: Do you believe that you will be able to converse well with this person into your old age? Everything else in marriage is transitory."
— Friedrich Nietzsche

"Love seems the swiftest, but it is the slowest of all growths. No man or woman really knows what perfect love is until they have been married a quarter of a century."
— Mark Twain

"Between man and wife even thoughts are contagious."
—Friedrich Nietzsche

"Whatever you may look like, marry a man your own age — as your beauty fades, so will his eyesight."
— Phyllis Diller

"Make your love as endless as your wedding ring."
— Lucius Annaeus Seneca

"The essence of a good marriage is respect for each other's personality combined with that deep intimacy, physical, mental, and spiritual, which makes a serious love between man and woman the most fructifying of all human experiences. Such love, like everything that is great and precious, demands its own morality, and frequently entails a sacrifice of the less to the greater; but such sacrifice must be voluntary, for, where it is not, it will destroy the very basis of the love for the sake of which it is made."
— Bertrand Russell

"It is love in old age, no longer blind, that is true love. For love's highest intensity doesn't necessarily mean its highest quality."
— Booth Tarkington

"What therefore God hath together joined, let not man put asunder."
— Mark 10:9

"Coupling doesn't always have to do with sex . . . [It is] two people holding each other up like flying buttresses. Two people depending on each other and babying each other and defending each other against the world outside. Sometimes it was worth all the disadvantages of marriage just to have that: one friend in an indifferent world."
— Erica Jong

"Marriages made in heaven are not exported."
— Samuel Hoffenstein

"Only choose in marriage a woman whom you would choose as a friend if she were a man."
— Joseph Joubert

"My definition of marriage . . . it resembles a pair of shears, so joined that they cannot be separated; often moving in opposite directions, yet always punishing anyone who comes between them."
— Sydney Smith

"The greatest ordeal in life is marriage; it is the central focus for enlightenment and the natural therapeutic process in the culture."

— Dr. Carl Whitiker

"Live so that when a man says he's married to you, he'll be boasting."

— Jim McMullan

"Marriage is either death or life; there is no betwixt and between."

— Kahlil Gibran

"Don't walk in front of me, I may not follow. Don't walk behind me, I may not lead; walk beside me, and be my friend."

— Irish proverb

"You know how I end relationships in New York now? I don't say, 'This isn't working out.' Or, 'I don't want to see you anymore.' I just say, 'You know, I love you . . . I want to marry you . . . I want to have your children. . .' Sometimes they make skid marks."

— Rita Rudner

"Marriage, as far as I'm concerned, is one of the most wonderful, heartwarming, satisfying experiences a human being can have. I've only been married seventeen years, so I haven't seen that side of it yet."
— George Gobel

"The bride wears white

"Marriage is something like the measles: we all have to go through it."

— Jerome K. Jerome

"Never get married in the morning. You never know who you might meet that night."

— Paul Hornung

ibolize purity. The groom wears black." ⁸⁹

— David Frost

"Marriage is popular because it combines the maximum of temptation with the maximum of opportunity."

— George Bernard Shaw

"The marriage state, with and without affection suitable to it, is the completest image of Heaven and Hell we are capable of receiving in this life."

— Sir Richard Steele

"Long engagements give people the opportunity of finding out each other's character before marriage, which is never advisable."

— Oscar Wilde

"When I was young I vowed never to marry until I found the ideal woman. Well, I found her — but alas, she was waiting for the ideal man."

— Robert Schumann

"Falling in love with someone is not necessarily a good starting point to getting married."
— Charles, Prince of Wales

"He tricked me into marrying him. He told me I was pregnant."
— Carol Leifer

"I love to cry at weddings, anybody's weddings, anytime . . . anybody's weddings, just so long as it's not mine!"
— Dorothy Fields

"I was married by a judge. I should have asked for a jury."

— Groucho Marx

"He marries best who p

"Do you know what it means to come home at night to a woman who'll give you a little love, a little affection, a little tenderness? It means you're in the wrong house!"
— Henny Youngman

"An archaeologist is the best husband any woman can have; the older they get the more interested he is in her."
— Agatha Christie

"Intellectuals should never marry. They won't enjoy it; and besides they should not reproduce themselves."
— Don Herold

"I think the best I can do is be a distraction."
— Jacqueline Bouvier Kennedy Onassis

off until it is too late."
— H.L. Mencken

"After marriage, husband and wife become two sides of a coin; they just can't face each other, but still they stay together."
— Hemant Joshi

" 'Tis my maxim, he's a fool that marries, but he's a greater fool that does not marry."
— William Wycherley

"Marriage is punishment for shoplifting in some countries."
— Mike Myers

"I've never yet met a man who could look after me. I don't need a husband. What I need is a wife."
— Joan Collins

"Marriage, well, I think of it as a marvelous thing for other people, like going to the stake."
— Anthony Thwaite

"Getting married is like getting into a tub of hot water. After you get used to it, it ain't so hot."
— Minnie Pearl

"The world has grown suspicious of anything that looks like a happily married life."
— Oscar Wilde

"Many a good hanging prevents a bad marriage."
——William Shakespeare

"Love is much better when you are not married."
— Maria Callas

"It is a woman's business to get married as soon as possible, and a man's to keep unmarried as long as he can."
— George Bernard Shaw

"The only really happy folk are married women and single men."
— H.L. Mencken

"You know what I did before I got married? Anything I wanted to."
— Henny Youngman

"Americans, who make
more of marrying for
love than any other
people, also break up
more of their marriages,
but the figure reflects not
so much the failure of
love as the determination
of people not to live
without it."

—— Morton Hunt

"God made man; God made woman. And when God found that men could not get along with women, God invented Mexico."
— Larry Storch

"I hate and regret the failure of my marriages. I would gladly give all my millions for just one lasting marital success."
— J. Paul Getty

"I have come to the conclusion never again to think of marrying, and for this reason, I can never be satisfied with anyone who would be blockhead enough to have me."
— Abraham Lincoln

"Many a man owes his success to his first wife and his second wife to his success."
— Jim Backus

"I don't worry about terrorism. I was married for two years."
— Sam Kinison

"I'd marry again if I found a man who had $15 million and would sign over half of it to me before the marriage, and guarantee he would be dead in a year."
— Bette Davis

"It was partially my fault we got divorced . . . I tended to place my wife under a pedestal."

— Woody Allen

"I've been married three times and each time I married the right person."

— Margaret Mead

"I'm the only man I know who has a marriage license made out 'To Whom It May Concern.'"

— Mickey Rooney

There once was an old man of Lyme
Who married three wives at a time.
When asked, "Why a third?"
He replied, "One's absurd!
And bigamy, Sir, is a crime!

— William Cosmo Monkhouse

"I belong to Bridegrooms Anonymous. Whenever I feel like getting married, they send over a lady in a housecoat and hair curlers to burn my toast for me."

— Dick Martin

"Where there is marriage without love, there will be love without marriage."

— Benjamin Franklin

"I've sometimes thought of marrying, and then I've thought again."

— Noel Coward

"A friend of mine was getting married and I bought her a subscription to *Modern Bride* magazine. The subscription laster longer than the marriage."

— Lily Tomlin

"Marriage is not a man's idea. A woman must have thought of it. Years ago some guy said, 'Let me get this straight, honey. I can't sleep with anyone else for the rest of my life, and if things don't work out you get to keep half my stuff? What a great idea.'"

— Bobby Slayton

"A bride at her second marriage does not wear a veil. She wants to see what she is getting."

— Helen Rowland

"I'm an excellent housekeeper. Every time I get a divorce I keep the house."

— Zsa Zsa Gabor

"When a man opens the car door for his wife, it's either a new car or a new wife."

— Prince Philip, Duke of Edinburgh

"Do not think about trying to make it through a lifetime with a man. Just concentrate on making it through a year . . . The reason a man will not try to split up with you after a year or so is his limitless fear of breaking in a new model."

— Stephanie Brush

"There is so little difference between husbands, you might as well keep the first."

— Adela Rogers St. Johns

"Anyone can see at a glance th
they do not love, they must lo

"Sometimes it takes pigheaded determination to hold a couple together; when that fails, a sense of humor really helps."
— Erma Bombeck

"Marriage is a lottery, but you can't tear up your ticket if you lose."
— F. M. Knowles

"Marriage is our last best chance to grow up."
— Joseph Barth

"Marriage is better than leprosy because it's easier to get rid of."
— W. C. Fields

"I guess the only way to stop divorce is to stop marriage."
— Will Rogers

"In our monogamous part of the world, to marry means to halve one's rights and double one's duties."
— Arthur Schopenhauer

"men and women marry those
ose they do not marry."

— Harriet Martineau

"For one human to love

another; that is perhaps the

most difficult of all tasks,

the ultimate, the last test

and proof, the work for

which all other work is

preparation."

— Rainer Maria Rilke

"The goal of our life should not be to find joy in marriage, but to bring more love and truth into the world. We marry to assist each other in this task. The most selfish and hateful life of all is that of two beings who unite in order to enjoy life. The highest calling is that of the man who has dedicated his life to serving God and doing good, and who unites with a woman in order to further that purpose."

— Leo Tolstoy

"May your joys be as deep as the oc

"Marriage is an Athenic wearing-together of families; of two souls with their individual fates and destinies of time and eternity — everyday life married to the timeless mysteries of the soul."

— Thomas Moore

"Strong are the instincts with which God has guarded the sacredness of marriage."

— Maria McIntosh

"Marriage is an act of will that signifies and involves a mutual gift, which unites the spouses and binds them to their eventual souls, with whom they make up a sole family — a domestic church."

— Pope John Paul II

"Marriages are made in Heaven."
— Alfred Lord Tennyson

"People talk about beautiful friendships between two persons of the same sex. What is the best of that sort, as compared with the friendship of man and wife, where the best impulses and highest ideals of both are the same. There is no place for comparison between the two friendships; the one is earthy, the other divine."

— Mark Twain

l your misfortunes as light as the foam."

— Irish proverb

"When perfect love and friendship are expressed between two souls, that love will be registered in heaven as one divine love; that love will be a commingled fount of love ever playing in the bosom of God. Divine love defies mortal destiny, and laughs at the impotency of time and death."

— Paramahansa Yogananda

"An ideal start for matrimony would be to have a drunken Rabbi perform a Catholic ceremony in an Episcopalian church. Then it could be declared illegal in the courts."

— W.C. Fields

"Many a marriage could have been saved if the couple had remembered this; that their hearts belong to each other but their souls belong to God."

— Lewis Evans

"Marriages are made in heaven, but so again are thunder and lightning."

— anonymous

"Live together in harmony, live together in love as though you had only one mind and one spirit between you. Never act from motives of personal vanity, but in humility think more of one another than you do of yourselves."

— Philippians 2:2-3

"It is only when we see marriage as a vehicle satisfy our unconscious yearnings."

"Look down, you gods, and on this couple drop a blessed crown."
— Shakespeare

"Seldom or never does a marriage develop into an individual relationship smoothly, without crisis. There is no birth of consciousness without pain."
— C. G. Jung

"Marriage is the mother of the world, and preserves kingdoms, and fills cities and churches, and heaven itself. Marriage, like the useful bee, builds a house, and gathers sweetness from every flower, and labors and unites into societies and republics and sends out colonies, and feeds the world with delicacies, and keeps order, and exercises many virtues, and promotes the interest of mankind, and is that state of good things to which God hath designed the present constitution of the world."
— Jeremy Taylor

"When men enter into the state of marriage they stand nearest to God."
— Henry Ward Beecher

"When you meet a man he is a stranger. When you marry him, he becomes your own self. When you quarrel, he becomes your enemy. It is your mind's attitude that determines what he is to you."
—Sri Nisargadatta Maharaj

nge and self-growth that we can begin to
— Harville Hendrix

index

about the authors...

Helene and Jim McMullan have been married for twenty-seven years. They have two sons, Sky and Tyson. Helene met Jim in 1968 while passing through Los Angeles. At the time, she was a singer/actress in a Broadway show and Jim was acting in films and television. Currently, Helene is a personal/professional "life" coach. Jim still acts (his best-known role was as Senator Dowling in *Dallas*). *Happily Ever After* is Helene's first book. Jim has written several others, including *Actors and Artists, Musicians as Artists, This Face of God, Instant Zen, Cheatin' Hearts, Broken Dreams and Stomped On Love* and *Hail to the Chief*. Helene and Jim live in Los Angeles, and still feel like newlyweds.

about the designer...

Dave Matli, who began working as a freelance designer and art director while in school at Art Center College of Design in Pasadena, California plans to make a career out of seeking simple, elegant solutions to visual communication problems. He has been happily married to Debbie Matli three years and will someday buy her a big house on an island.